AMPHIBIANS

Maria Koran

EYEDISCOVER

EYEDISCOVER

Go to www.eyediscover.com and enter this book's unique code.

BOOK CODE

AVG68939

EYEDISCOVER brings you optic readalongs that support active learning.

Published by AV^2 by Weigl
350 5th Avenue, 59th Floor New York, NY 10118
Website: www.eyediscover.com

Library of Congress Cataloging-in-Publication Data available on request

ISBN 978-1-4896-8045-7 (hardcover)

Printed in Guangzhou, China
1 2 3 4 5 6 7 8 9 0 23 22 21 20 19

072019
121818

Project Coordinator: John Willis
Designer: Mandy Christiansen and Ana María Vidal

Weigl acknowledges Getty Images, iStock, and Minden Pictures as the primary image suppliers for this title.

EYEDISCOVER provides enriched content, optimized for tablet use, that supplements and complements this book. EYEDISCOVER books strive to create inspired learning and engage young minds in a total learning experience.

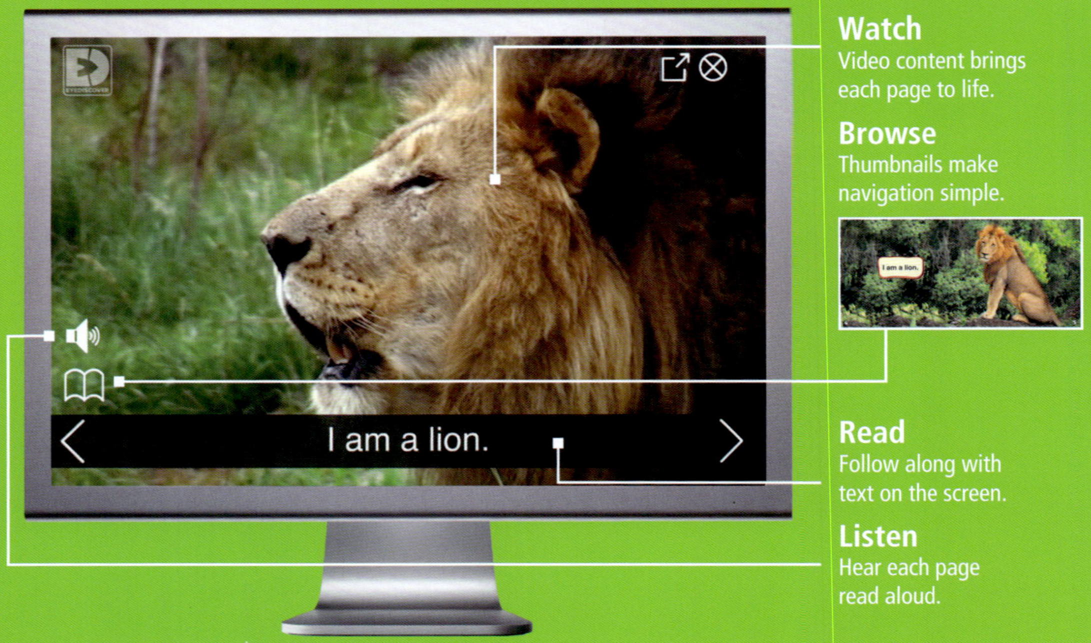

Your EYEDISCOVER Optic Readalongs come alive with...

Audio
Listen to the entire book read aloud.

Video
High resolution videos turn each spread into an optic readalong.

OPTIMIZED FOR

- ✓ TABLETS
- ✓ WHITEBOARDS
- ✓ COMPUTERS
- ✓ AND MUCH MORE!

AMPHIBIANS

In this book, you will learn about

- what they are
- what they look like
- what they do

and much more!

Amphibians spend the first part of their lives in water.

6

Amphibians change as they grow. Many spend the second part of their lives on land.

Many amphibians live near water. They breathe and drink through their smooth skin.

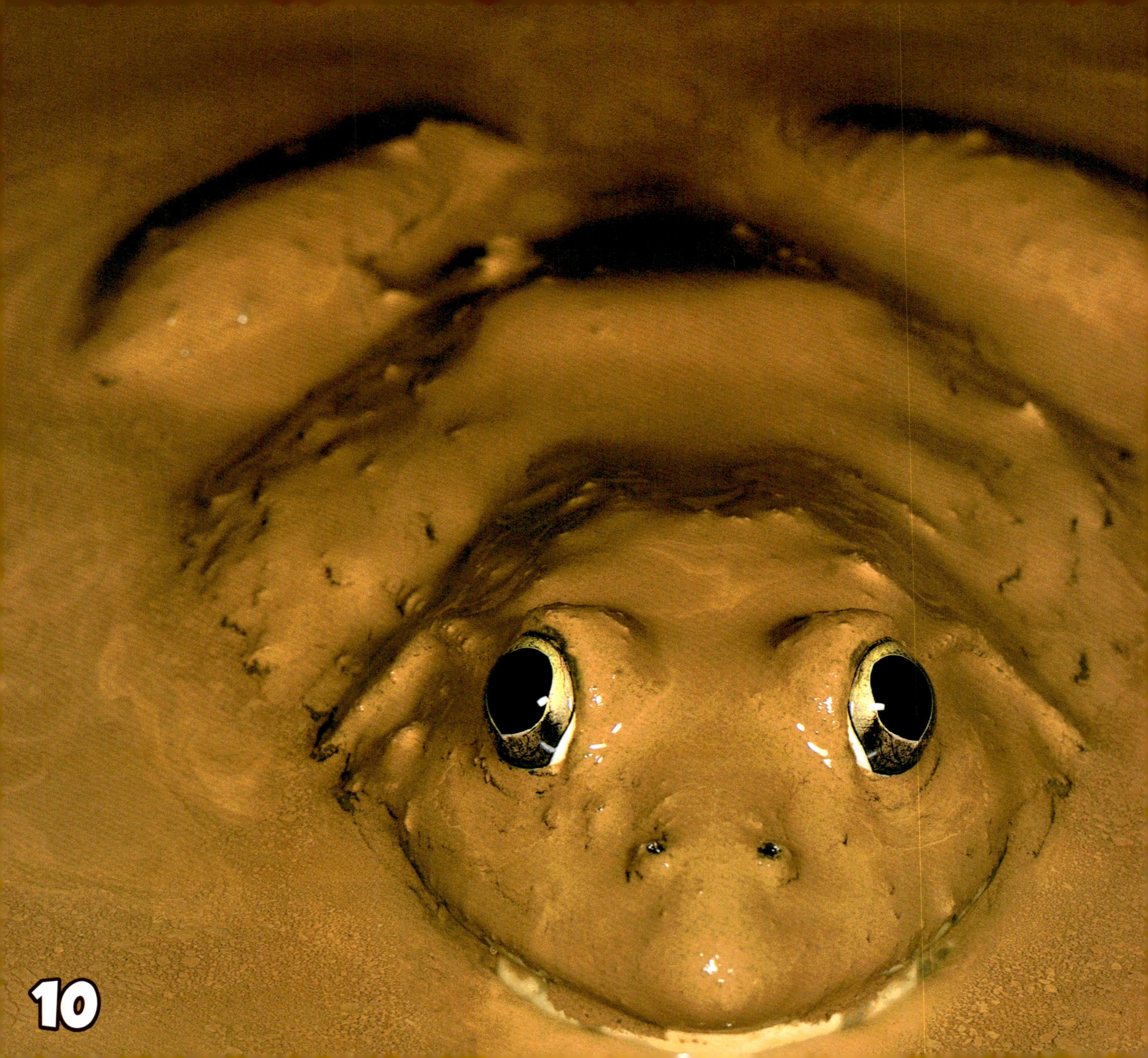

Some amphibians sit on rocks to keep warm. Others bury themselves in mud.

Salamanders are amphibians. They can grow back lost body parts.

Some salamanders spend their whole lives underwater. They breathe using gills on their heads.

Frogs and toads are also amphibians. A group of frogs is called an army.

Most frogs use their long tongues to catch and eat food.

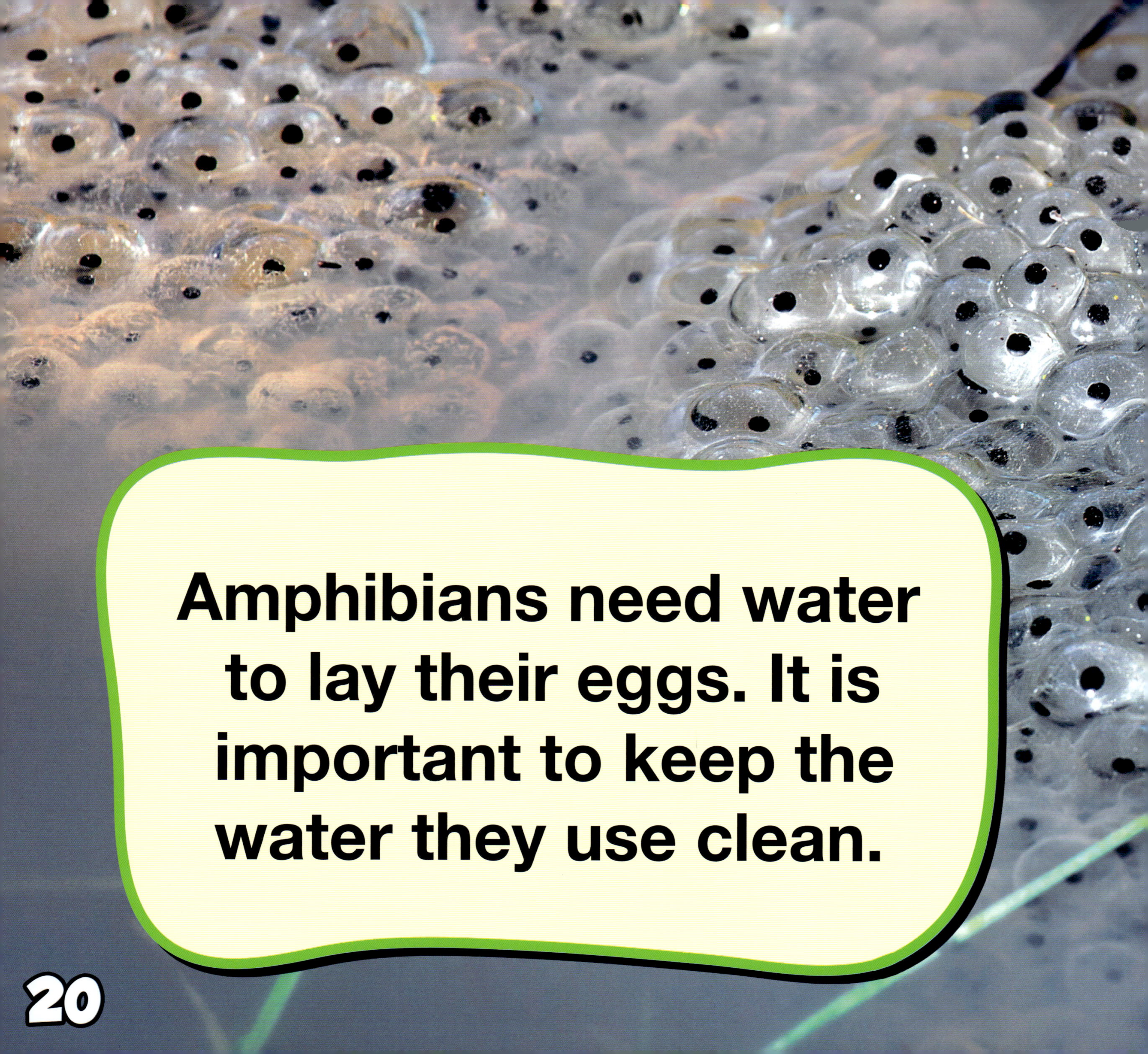

Amphibians need water to lay their eggs. It is important to keep the water they use clean.

AMPHIBIANS BY THE NUMBERS

A bullfrog can lay up to 20,000 eggs at a time.

There are more than 6,500 kinds of amphibians.

Amphibians first appeared on Earth more than 300 million years ago.

The **largest** salamanders can be **more than 5 feet** long. (1.5 meters)

Goliath frogs are the **heaviest** frogs. They can weigh more than **7 pounds.** (3 kilograms)

Caecilians are **amphibians** that often live **underground.** They do not have **any** legs.

KEY WORDS

Research has shown that as much as 65 percent of all written material published in English is made up of 300 words. These 300 words cannot be taught using pictures or learned by sounding them out. They must be recognized by sight. This book contains 40 common sight words to help young readers improve their reading fluency and comprehension. This book also teaches young readers several important content words, such as proper nouns. These words are paired with pictures to aid in learning and improve understanding.

Page	Sight Words First Appearance
4	first, in, lives, of, part, the, their, water
7	as, change, land, many, on, grow, second, they
9	and, near, through
11	keep, others, some, to
12	are, back, can
15	heads
16	a, also, an, group, is
18	eat, food, long, most, use
20	important, it, need

Page	Content Words First Appearance
4	amphibians
9	skin
11	mud, rocks
12	salamanders
15	gills
16	army, frogs, toads
18	tongues
20	eggs

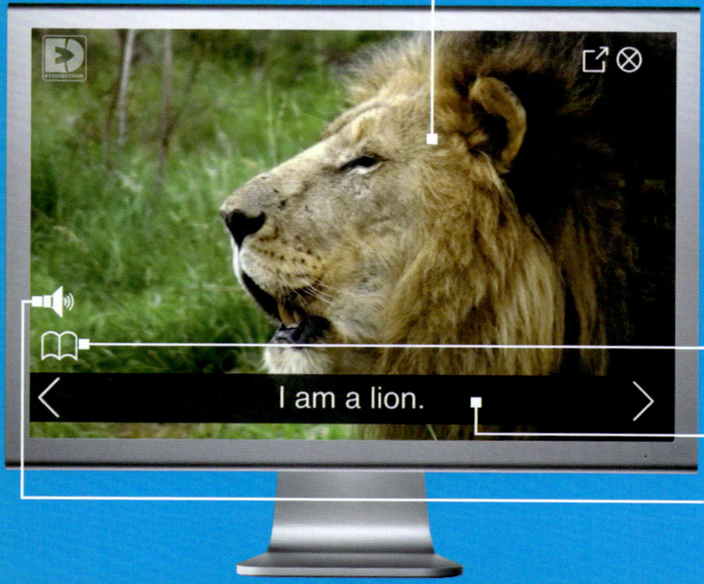

Watch
Video content brings each page to life.

Browse
Thumbnails make navigation simple.

Read
Follow along with text on the screen.

Listen
Hear each page read aloud.

EYEDISCOVER

Go to www.eyediscover.com and enter this book's unique code.

BOOK CODE

AVG68939